Charleston
In
Poetry
and Photographs

by a Native Charlestonian...

Lorraine Shea Rich

Dearest Bob, Wendy,
Kendra, Keri -
We hope you enjoy
these snapshots of our
home town - We can't
wait to share it with
you!
Margaret, Roxanna,
Harper, Hannah

6-01

Pen to Paper Publications
P.O. Box 31573, Charleston, S.C. 29417
email: pentopaper@fwb.gulf.net

FIRST EDITION
1998

Printed in the United States of America

ISBN 0-9662776-0-0

Acknowledgements

I thank my husband, Ralph, for his untiring devotion to this labor of love, his photographic perception, and for his (right up to the last detail) assistance in this publication.

I would also like to thank George Cash for his technical and artistic expression of the poems and photographs set before him.

My mother, Elizabeth Jensen Shea, is to be credited for the collection of timeless photographs seen throughout the book of myself, my siblings, and other relatives. She has also been my ceaseless mentor.

And, Nancy Shea Sirigos, my sister, is thanked for her editing and her photo of the Old Bridge taken from Mount Pleasant. It was a rainy, foggy day, and she really captured the spirit within.

To the rest of my family, thank you for your inspiration, and Nanny, you live forever in my heart.

Photographs by:

Ralph Thomas Rich
Lorraine Shea Rich
Elizabeth Jensen Shea
Nancy Shea Sirigos

Edited by:

Nancy Shea Sirigos

Production:

George Cash
Ralph Thomas Rich

CONTENTS

CHARLESTON, MY CHARLESTON

And home isn't a house,
but a town and a memory,
of porches with houses attached,
with balconies and sea breezes
that tug on drapes leading to long foyers.

Shutters closed to an afternoon sun.
Shaded rooms resting in evening shadows.
Mansions left over from wars,
passed down with a heritage.

Historical buildings painted in hues of rainbow,
fronted by palms, facing cobbled streets.

Visitors envision gray uniformed men,
whisper from open carriages,
while nannies stroll their charges to waterfront parks.

Four Corners of Law, Exchange Building, the Cathedral
fill up city blocks, a pleasant walk from the Market,
where sweetgrass and flowers are twisted and bunched
into baskets, bouquets,
examined and sold,
where slaves were the items a few lifetimes ago.

Fort Sumter silently floats
against the watchful battery of homes.
And the lineage of those who died against,
now reside side by side.

Wrought iron fences, gates and cannons,
are hand traced and climbed by our children,
as were they by their parents, and those before,
and those before...

And these old trees hold the secrets.
How I love, I know so well,
these hallowed streets where history speaks.
My cornerstone, my home,
my home.

And my spirit soars where the moss flows
and the moss flows, and flows,
how the moss does flow.

MARKET NEAR MEETING

I stood and watched
the silent figure bend and twist,
wrap, pull, and tug sweetgrass and palmetto
into sweetgrass, Gullah baskets
in Carolina sun shadows

Red clay walls
ballasted by columns,
framed by the brickened façade,
wrought iron arches twisted into banisters
flanked by gas lamps

If this market could speak
as we walk through yesterday's streets
how would it sound,
what would it say

Standing firm in today
watching them set up stalls of goods on Market near Meeting
my mind retreats into days long gone
for I know that the shifting sand is ageless

Though time is measured and day is toned
now the same as it was then,
my mind's eye sees ringing chimes,
hears shades of voices, days of old

But these southern ways remain the same,
pulled, tugged and stored,
and wrapped in its warmth,
weaving the magic of now and of then
into the sweetest and strongest
and finest of blends

RAINBOW ROW

you stroke the city in shadows of hue
your palate aged, tints of rose, beige,
touched with the clearest shades of blue,
profiled in timelessness,

you are the poetry
breezes, the song
the measure to be played sweet,
allegro, andante, allegretto,
by decade, by degrees,

pastelled in historical rote
I hear you, note by silent note

penned and poemed, Rainbow Row
seasoned, smoothed, dulcet
soft, the gentle stroke

MAY PROCESSION

"Tis the month of our Mother
the blessed and beautiful May..."

Soft resounding stanzas floated,
while cherubs rounded the sandstone.

White dotted swiss, puffy ivory sleeves,
grograine ribbon tied in bows,
wound around tiny waists.

White gloved hands pulled and tugged
at netted veils and baby's breath,
loomed in strands of runaway curls.

Little men in little suits
shiny hair combed into place
restless feet in scuffed white shoes

Miniature brides and miniature grooms,
dangled rosaries in pressed together hands.

Bouquets of flowers gripped against chests.

Rosy cheeked faces mirrored
the black robed nuns,
warning, gesturing, and dashing
from the tiny to the not
in our bastion of piety.

The prisms of stained glass
effused with light
bells pealed; the lofty organ thundered to life.

White gloves wet with Holy Water
In the Name of the Father,
and of the Son,
and of the Holy Ghost,
Amen.

The congregation turned
as echoes shuffled down the marble floor,
when the Bishop raised his staff
and we Processed and we Professed,
filing through the holy land
of Broad Street's Cathedral.

And, we paused to genuflect,
one by one to place with grace
now wilted bouquets
at the Statue of Our Lady.

ST. PHILIP'S BELLS

Whose spirits live in the eaves of Saint Philip's
pulling the bells we hear as we stroll?
Names covered in shadows from the masonry tower
once plotted and placed near the streets far below

arched windows, pillared stone
the somber tower
courts, it hones, gifts us as we walk the farthest streets
yet who lies in sweet repose,
who lies beneath our feet

You, who led our nation:
Mr. John C. Calhoun, 1782 - 1850
Vice President

Words for freedom, poised and penned,
Independence signed, and thus proclaimed,
his life, pursuit, was freedom,
this, his noble name:
Mr. Edward Rutledge, 1749 - 1800

dear remembered, dear remembered
sweet remembered lifted soul

whose spirits pull the bells
we know their words so well

*"When in the Course of human events
it becomes necessary for one people
to dissolve the political bands..."*

earth, the bed where these, our heroes lie,
would they not have come before us,
how would we now abide

SCENTS, SENSES, AND SPRING

leaves rustle
and the carillon chime

palms shudder
and bells sound

whiffs of magnolia
honeysuckle, tea roses
crape myrtle,
camellias, jessamine

the warm mellifluous calm
stirred in an afternoon breeze

as fragrance winds
down city streets
the bells from steeples peal

COLONIAL LAKE

Stately colonialistic homes
donning steeples, dormer windows
encased, surrounded by porches,
adorned with columns,
nestle on Rutledge Avenue
emerge reflective in mill pond glass

Framed, renamed, Colonial Lake
her diminutive stature edged by palms,
adorned by benches,
lined with azaleas, oleanders

Crabbing lines are furled into lapping gray waters
of this floating home to gulls, this gentle quiet oasis,
our land locked gathering hole
feasting on sun, quiet, a slower pace
city block of country filled quaintness

The sameness of then, now
changes few, mirrored in photographs
and folklores of the past.
While palmettos belie the years
in their shadows' steady growth

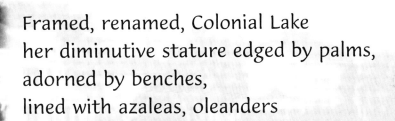

KERRISONS

The old general store,
two doors down from the livery stable,
housing wares of food, romanticized, immortalized,
harmonized in small towns.

My favorite in Charleston was not so small,
not so quaint, not so pallid,
but tasteful, refined, historical...

A façade of glass turns the eyes and the frame follows
to press brass handles, to enter the din
of heady leathered fragrances from purses, satchels, belts,
the air now sprinkled with waves of perfumes
decanters gently pressed from table topped displays.

Muted heels tap lightly, clip over polished wooden floors
co-mingled with quiet conversation.

Mirrored walls, beams, vaulted ceilings stagger
subdue, echo the mercantile rituals,
as patrons and clerks visit while vacuumed tubes are exhumed,
tender rendered.

Steps reach the uniformed figure, gates pull,
"going up", the white gloved hand turns,
evokes the whir and grind, the smile southern,
the view now changed.
"Third Floor, Women's Wear, Lingerie
watch your step, please."

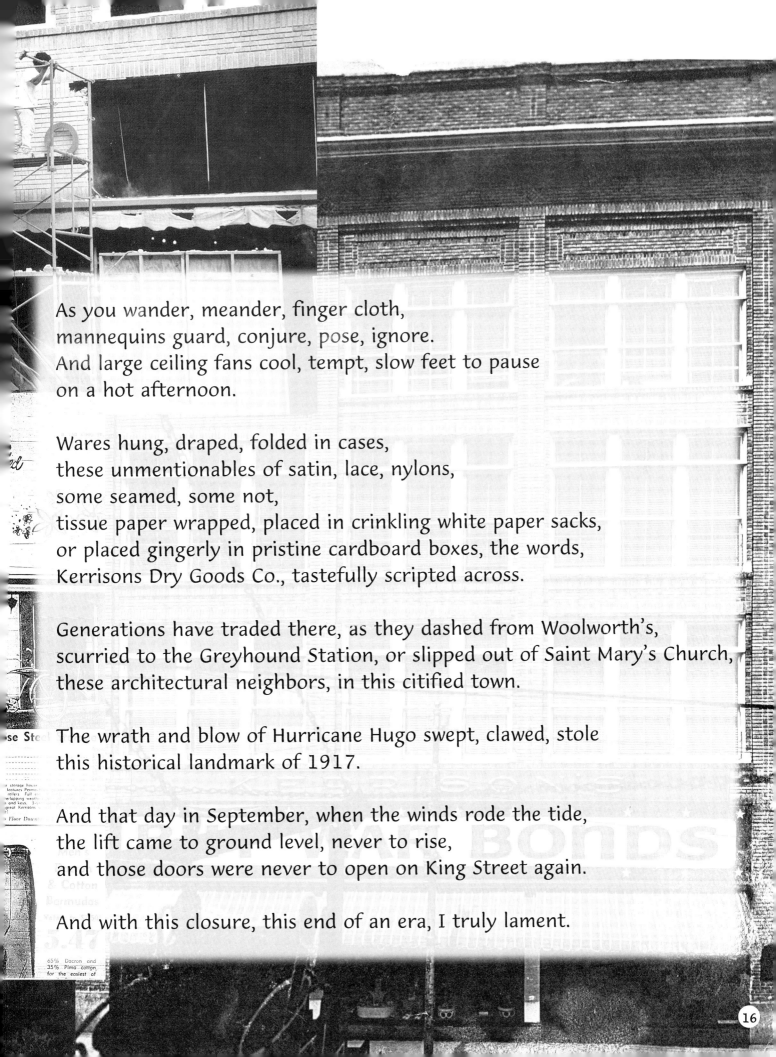

As you wander, meander, finger cloth,
mannequins guard, conjure, pose, ignore.
And large ceiling fans cool, tempt, slow feet to pause
on a hot afternoon.

Wares hung, draped, folded in cases,
these unmentionables of satin, lace, nylons,
some seamed, some not,
tissue paper wrapped, placed in crinkling white paper sacks,
or placed gingerly in pristine cardboard boxes, the words,
Kerrisons Dry Goods Co., tastefully scripted across.

Generations have traded there, as they dashed from Woolworth's,
scurried to the Greyhound Station, or slipped out of Saint Mary's Church,
these architectural neighbors, in this citified town.

The wrath and blow of Hurricane Hugo swept, clawed, stole
this historical landmark of 1917.

And that day in September, when the winds rode the tide,
the lift came to ground level, never to rise,
and those doors were never to open on King Street again.

And with this closure, this end of an era, I truly lament.

SUMMER KIDS

there ain't no buggers out tonight
cause daddy killed em all last night

it was summertime
the only cool an occasional chill
as beaded skin dried
and we breathlessly crouched behind maples, oaks
and all those sinewy pines

we were all crew tops, flat tops, pig and pony tails
unaware and unabashed
clad in summer-worn, shoulder-tied sun suits,
faded shorts, and hand me down shirts
elbows and knees boasting yesterday's scrapes
barefoot and bold, cleaned but not yet ready for bed

the air was thick with crickets, tree frogs, giggles and squeals
fireflies, mosquitoes
magnolias and tea roses
marinating in a Charleston night

neighborhood silence was loosely threaded with shouts of
I GOT YOU
YOU DID NOT
I'M TELLIN MOM

but she was well aware and on the porch
rocking our cotton diapered sibling to sleep
as we skirted through moon shadows
playing
there ain't no buggers out tonight
cause daddy killed em all last night

THE CITADEL

The thread of gray
twisted through the annals of time
ranks of wool, men of steel

the tapestry ever changing

gray and the blue
posted guards, cannons fired
blood was lost, war began
the city undone,
so turns the weave

the fabric of our heritage
torn and stitched by the hands of steel,
so the thread of gray

men served the country, women served the men
but men were sworn, born to as men,
so blends the weave

tradition feels the thread
knots pulled loose,
and statutes change the ranks
but the buttressed bulwark remains
our CITADEL

the needle threads
the ranks have split
mended together
stitch by stitch

the sentinel now a woven blend
Confederates bowed to change again
in union united women and men
to have and to hold from this day forward
strength to keep this land

and freedom will ring

echo the bells
echo the bells
echo the bells
of change

HAMPTON PARK

Before they started saying
"don't feed the animals",
they sold peanuts
at the snack stand at the zoo.

I remember...

Our tiny hands would reach into the paper sack
pinching dried shelled treats,
placing them into the long hairy monkey fingers
lacing through iron bars.

Primate lips moving every which way,
they screeched, cackled,
and dragged their rough bottomed rears
to plop on wet cement, where they groomed, watching us.

We'd skip down the path to the Park's beloved legacy,
the tonnage of gray leathery skin truncating his way,
till distanced within reach he'd manage to inhale
the remainder of peanuts, shells,
tickling my skin with his vacuumed breath.

Wide eyed and open mouthed,
I retraced my last step,
my moist nuzzled hand reaching for mom's.

The rest of the afternoon mom watched
as we mimicked monkeys, from low limb
aged live oaks.

...And then

on Easter Sunday, after Mass,
exchanging "monkey see, monkey do" for decorum,
we'd hunt spottable eggs.

By mid-afternoon we were content
with hand holding, our energy long spent.

We strolled through the expanse of rose gardens,
unnoticed by the white swans mirrored in the pond
my home-made lavender dress faded in contrast
to the display of azaleas, tulips, crape myrtle, hyacinths, wisteria.
Our shaded walk thick with fragrance.

Oftentimes baseball sounds
drifted through the parking lot,
escaping from the diamond down the street.

I don't remember Hampton Park
never being collaged in my life's fullness,
but, I do remember running, climbing,
and filling enough blossom-filled afternoons
to hold me through the winters
of many years to come.

THE VEGETABLE MAN

"Frush okry
plump tomatoes,
yello squash
young potatoes

Sivey beans, scrung beans,
blue-
berries, strawberries..."

He reached our doorstep
long after his song.

His frame bent.
The cart held by roughened, weathered hands,
you'd see his coal colored skin glistening.
A bent straw hat shading dark eyes,
in the baked, breezeless noonday sun.

His melody, his wares drifted through our streets.
The vegetable man offering his fruits,
earthy bunches of vegetables, and a song.

Little did he know his fragrances, colors,
music would bathe in my senses.
They've fed me these many years now gone.

So, I linger in my memory in mid afternoon.
Wait for him to turn the corner
as I listen for...
"Vegtbles, I got BaNanas, Tendr young ...."

24

SPOLETO

Mimes thunder through silence
amid colors of tumbling, juggling balls,
and music spins through spring soaked sunshine,
with child giggles and wide-eyed wonder.

Stories leap through laces of mid afternoon shadows,
stringed and drummed, clanged, fluted,
floating in sing-songy, open ended verse.

Edged to knees on quilted magic carpets,
cushioned by soon to be summer lawns, they marvel,
children young, and young at heart,
resplendent with evening filled culture
still spinning in mind's eyes.

Spoleto has danced into our hearts, and we measure its beat,
its rhythm, sway to its soul, in colors,
as it moves through our streets,
ablaze, in music, with dances, dreams.

Oh, Spoleto!
The look, the feel, the taste of it.
How delicious, how magic you are.

"SUNDAY MORNING NEWS AND COURIER"

The strong clear voice called,
music filled the sky with
"Sunday Morning News and Courier",
get your *"Sunday Morning News and Courier..."*
This,
before the shadows lifted,
while the bird song was full in early daylight.
Papers carried door to door, neighbor to neighbor.

My mind is hungry for yesterday's news,
quieter times.

Those days when red-faced, displaced northern priests
offered southern summer twelve o'clock Mass,
chanting Latin verses, above hand bells ringing,
while *Gloria in Excelsis Deo*,
Sanctus, Sanctus..
lifted
Stained glass windows thrown open,
filling the incense clouded room with outside sounds
our prayers wafting through Ansonborough's streets.

St. Joseph's full of sensible shoed women
tapping the expanse of wooden floor.
Their summer hats firm on bowed heads.
Our chapel caps secured with bobby pins,
square in the middle.
One white gloved hand slowly waving a cardboard fan
the other pressing rosary beads,
while one or two of us drifted, slowly fainting,
in the ceaseless, humid southern heat.

Chilled ham, potato salad, chocolate cake waiting
for the fasted to feast on return.

I miss those simpler days,
of three channels, one paper, quiet streets, Sunday drivers.

And, I can't help but try to remember
the sound of his voice, the tune of his song...
"I have your
Sunday Morning News and Courier..."

AUNT JULIE'S RED RICE

Found an old recipe
on a folded card
the words faded, blended and smudged

```
take one bell pepper diced, an onion, bacon or ham
2 cups of tomatoes and juices all boiled in a pan
add one cup rice, cook 20 minutes or
till the rice is done
and the liquid is gone
```

and...
it's summer afternoon at Uncle Buddy's,
the family reunion and I can smell Aunt Julie's Red Rice

our softball game's third inning
and my cousin, Fran's, crisp swing and
whack
Roy leans over the wall, peeks in the graveyard
followed by the others, eager wide-eyed
as small hands hang on, dangling feet in old dirty tennis shoes

"it's there on the tombstone," someone whispers
spooky, and in the heat, we shiver
the bravest runs to retrieve it before we are discovered
by our mothers and their mothers,
sitting in the shade in kitchen chairs
with aunts, nieces, and wives of their brothers
in cotton dresses, shapeless, sleeveless
their feet tired, crossed, and resting

their hushed, melodious tones
float above the smell of dinner

those faces so much the same,
a few weathered by time
so many framed in wisps of hair faded gray
stories shared where Spanish moss
swoops and glides, limb over limb
lower then lower
as we climbed higher and higher in aged oaks
with honeysuckle on our breath

I often ache for one taste of yesterday
slow served meals
in the breezeless summer sun
to rest in those open arms
pressed against those warm bosoms

seasoned memories and recipes
were handed down
from gentle hands

and I often cook Aunt Julie's red rice.
Yet, it always needs something, needs something
uumm, it needs something

COOPER RIVER BRIDGES

Mighty monarchical towers of strength
two crowns anointed
gatekeepers
potentates on stilted gait
on massive thrones
with structured majesty

Skies of thunder
blood fire at night
in the visage of a liquid dawn
we wind through your massive limbs
heart of steel, frame of stone

Through lofty spans
we soar above the earth
to breach the waters
beneath your spiraled girth

SHEM CREEK

Cawing of gulls dot the rhythm
of wires and masts clanking,
evoking a blessing of sea and sky.

Sounds hold a smell, a shape of their own
of salty reeds, shrimp, bait.

Birds hover, perched on piers silently watching, waiting
as vessels saunter, pour into channels,
moor into slips, dragging vaulted profiles
through ebbing waters

Sea drenched wooden piers moan with muted steps.
Air thickens with hushed voices
while cargo is gathered, hoisted, heaved to shore.

Misty fog stirs the air,
blends with distant skies now spilled with gold, violet, rose.

Night settles, covers diffused shadows,
silent, still, waiting for morning light

For the calming sounds at daybreak
as shrimp boats etch through glassy stillness,
trailing silken wakes,
while they waltz, dip, sway
to the caw of the gulls.

THE FOGGER MAN

Then there was the summer Susan was twelve, I ten,
and it rained for six weeks.
We were at Nanny's, and Donald was just six months old.

The fogger man would come by at dusk,
in between showers.
We would run when we heard his truck;
arms waving, dashing ahead of billowing clouds of gray.

Nanny would draw our bath,
and one by one we'd submerge, to return squeaky clean,
and cotton clad in nightclothes.
Pigtails dripping down our backs,
we'd climb into the porch swing,
hunker down close as we could to Nanny.

One grandchild on her lap,
bookened in the middle,
she would spin stories
till the moon shadows filled the lawn.

Two sets of toes touching the gray slabs of wood,
we were lulled to peaceful silence
fanned by the breeze from the waterway.

Prayers said and bedded down,
we'd squiggle and squirm for space
in the old wooden double bed,
lying in the darkness kicking off sheets.

Ships and barges would weave through the sandbars,
led by the slow moan of the buoy
and the beam from Sullivan's Island Lighthouse,
on Station 20.

I toured it once, the Lighthouse,
with Mom's Cub Scout troop.
The ladder led straight up into the sky.

But, that was the summer Donald was two and a half.
It didn't rain much that year,
and the fogger man,
well, I guess he just stayed home.

THIS LITTLE PIGGY

Skittering feet bare and tanned
lick thick, cool summer lawn
catching long loose clovers in curled up toes.

Straddling jutted roots from the chinaberry tree,
they bathe in showers as dandelion seeds
are turned in circles and fall,
flake upon flake.

Stubbed on the edge of the old railroad post,
they climb, balance, lean and sway on the chain fence;
leap, then crunch on solid dark earth far below.

A skip and a crawl as Simon says,
to Island's end,
where plums and blackberries
are picked, licked and plopped
into song rhyming mouths.

Reeds snap, crunch, and groan
as pluff mud squishes through little child toes.

Fiddlers run, gulls cry and boats moan.
Nanny calls.
Says "its dinner time."

And those bare feet fly
all the way home.

SULLIVAN'S ISLAND
AND NANNY

Her gray streaked hair pinned in a bun,
a few loose strands lifted in a breeze.

In a soft cotton dress,
worn shoes on stockinged feet,
she walks across the wooden porch
holding two glasses of sweet iced tea.

The old rocking chair creaks
as she slides into its well-worn seat.

We share the same eyes, small chin, quiet disposition,
and
small talk about the day, the news, our friends.

There's damp clothes rolled up in the refrigerator
right next to the cookie dough.
She'll bake while ironing this afternoon.

Sheets thunder and slap on the clothesline.
The once slow wind's picking up.
It smells like it's going to rain.

From the kitchen we hear the crabs we caught,
clawing and scrambling
in the galvanized tub.

Dinner

The buoy on the waterway moans— a barge silently glides by,
sailboat following in her wake,
rocking in the choppy spray.

How can years ago feel and taste like yesterday?

I feel the breeze, remember the feel.
See Nanny rocking on her old wooden porch,
still leaning in her love
with my arms around my knees

SEP
55

MID DAY REPAST

Dried, so dried, peanut butter
thinly sandwiched between white bread.
Milk, room temperatured in wax cartons,
the platform from which a caterpillar leaps,
plops, drowns in; as I fall through the monkey bars,
uniformed, sand coated.
Reminded that girls should remember to be ladies.
And Simon says, halls echo, bananas brown,
in recycled, used to be "used again," lunch bags.

Waxed paper covered cowboy cookies coax,
remind me of school buses, cursive penmanship.
I won a dollar for: and A is for Agriculture, B is for Bismarck, I think.
While C is for Cotton, D is for Dried Peanut Butter Sandwiches.
Ashes to ashes, we all fall down.
Down the memory,
echoes those chambers, bouncing off walls,
in the halls in my mind,
Past black robes, sailboats, whiter than snow,
as white as black is black;
girls should always remember to be ladies.
This caterpillar...now a butterfly,
floating through moments in Stella Maris Elementary,
or was it Blessed Sacrament, when I bolted into Sister Who's It,
the one holding the sign that screamed, "walk."
A moment of silence...please, a moment.
While I get the peanut butter off the roof of my mind.

SKY LINE

From the rugged surface of silver sparkled rocks
surrounded by sea oats, shells, sand and sky
I follow the porpoise as it flirts and skims
in the wake of the shrimp boat
newly launched from its harbor and haven at Shem Creek

sea gulls and pelicans join the passage
to lunge and dip, purging fish from the wild running surf

tangled waves thrust and collide
the sparkled gray jetty left soaked now
as I

connected to life by a silhouette
the Harbor of Charleston
full-framed in my view
from lands end on Sullivan's Island

The winter wind whips my sandy legs
so I continue my cat walk along the jetty shore
pausing as gulls call and porpoises leap
and buoys moan
and waves heave to the thunder of life...

CHARLESTON BY GAS LIGHT

You look so lovely in the flicker of lamplight.
There's a gentle hue through the fire's glow.
Though it has been years since I've lived here,
the years have been good,
and it shows.

I am touched,
so very pleased.
You transcend time with grace,
with ease.
Your changes, I see, adding dignity.

There's something about the lamplight,
and, yet, add to the flickering glow,
your radiant warmth,
that old Southern charm.

You are loved, dear Charleston,
and, it shows.

About the Author

Lorraine is a native of Charleston and spends as much time as possible here with her family.

Although previously featured in several publications through the Southern Poetry Review, this selection of poetry has been written solely for this, her first book, for this her first love, Charleston.